MOTOR CARS *and*
SERV-US STATIONS

William D. Jones

Motor Cars and SERVUS STATIONS

WILLIAM D. JONES

Jones Photo Co.
Professional Photographers
1918 Simpson Avenue
Aberdeen, WA 98520
(360) 532-8940

ISBN 0-9666342-0-9

Library of Congress Catalog Card Number 98-073202

Cover and Book Design: Kathy Campbell
Photo scanning: Amy McCroskey

Printed by Gorham Printing, Rochester, Washington USA

DEDICATION

To "Zook"
> My wife, Marzella, over 53 years

To our six children
> Ruth, Paul, Barbara, David, Greg and Karen

Our Grandchildren and Great-Grandchildren

To my two sisters
> Helen Jones Gill and Jaqueline Jones Lusier

My mother, Ruth Monteith Jones
> Who I had for only 12 years

& Dad, Bliss B. Jones, who took most of the photographs

ACKNOWLEDGMENTS

To all the people who have encouraged me to publish these photographs as a history of the motor car and service stations where the customer was met by an attendant and really *served us*. I say thanks.

A special thanks to Amy McCroskey, Kurt Gorham and Kathy Campbell of Gorham Printing, for all their help and suggestions.

From the days of the song *Daisy and a Bicycle Built for Two* to *In My Merry Oldsmobile*, the Motor Car was responsible for setting the course of life in the twentieth century.

BLISS B. JONES

Motor Cars and SERV-US STATIONS

Some of the first gasoline powered vehicles were dreamed up by the mechanics in bicycle or buggy shops, motorizing both horse drawn carriages and two or three wheeled cycles. Before 1907, the proud owner of a gasoline propelled conveyance had to carry an extra container of fuel to guarantee that he would be able to make the return trip home. A gas station was unheard of until that time and the driver of a horseless carriage really pushed his luck in hoping that another vehicle owner might be willing to spare some of his gas supply.

Country driving was probably more risky for refill availability than in the towns or cities where automobile dealers and repair garages were springing up as fast as the inventions were being improved on. About 1910, the first underground storage tanks were installed so fuel could be pumped directly into the vehicle fuel tank. Single curbside pumps were being installed in front of almost any type store, be it city or country and sometimes two or three different businesses in the same block.

In 1913 the first modern "Serv-Us" station was introduced in Pittsburgh, Pennsylvania, where off-street pumps and other automobile services were available—oil and tire pressure were checked and the windshield washed.

Branded gasoline made its appearance a short time before, so customers started faithfully refueling at their favorite brand station, staffed by uniformed attendants under big porcelain trademark signs. Every town had at least one company station of each of the major gasoline brands in the territory. A driver could pull up to the pump of his choice and sit there behind the wheel while the attendant pumped the gas, checked the oil and battery, washed the windows and anything else that the customer wanted. In addition, it was not unusual to receive a free road map or lithographic scenic posters suitable for framing, all for a fill-up of your favorite brand of gas.

The year that the first off-street genuine service station opened in 1913, my two generations of professional photographers, (my grandfather who started in photography in 1880 in Silverton, Oregon and my father who was born in the business in 1892) moved from Oregon to Grays Harbor County, Washington. Grandpa opened a portrait studio in Hoquiam, Washington that year and Dad bought out a commercial and photofinishing studio in Aberdeen, Washington in 1914. We are now in the fourth generation and have been photographing people and other subjects, including automobile and service stations in the Northwest for more than 83 years.

This is a collection of the automobile, the service

stations, the oil companies and related memorabilia, before the Self-Serv, back when it was Serv-Us Stations.
We hope you enjoy some nostalgic hours.

Greg Jones

William L. Jones

Bliss B. Jones

William D. Jones

GRAY MOTOR CAR
ENDURANCE RUN. The
manufacturer didn't have proving
grounds like they do today, so if a
dealer (in this case M. M.
Stewart), could come up with
some challenge and get
photographs, the company would
pay for any expenses plus a bonus.
This was in 1919 fording Conner
Creek in Grays Harbor County,
Washington. For this event M. M.
Stewart was paid $200.00 from
the factory. Probably the
photographer got $5.00. The shop
foreman shellacked all the wiring
so the car wouldn't stall.

OLYMPIC HIGHWAY from
Copalis Crossing to
Humptulips on the way to
Lake Quinault in the
Olympic National Park.
Chehalis County (now Grays
Harbor County), 1917.

Photo No. 3500

The Roaring 20s

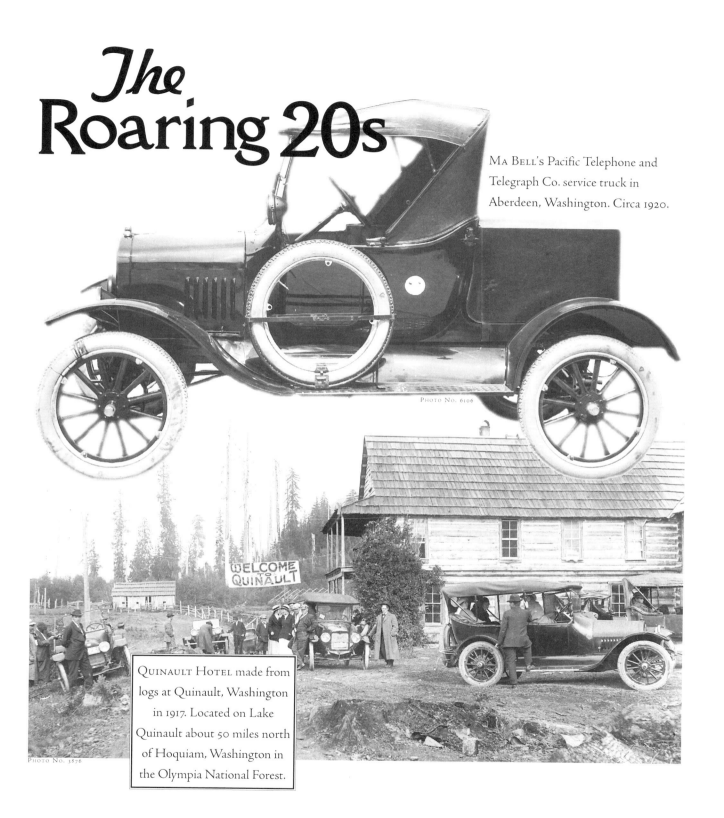

Ma Bell's Pacific Telephone and Telegraph Co. service truck in Aberdeen, Washington. Circa 1920.

Photo No. 6106

Photo No. 3876

QUINAULT HOTEL made from logs at Quinault, Washington in 1917. Located on Lake Quinault about 50 miles north of Hoquiam, Washington in the Olympia National Forest.

HARRY THOMPSON'S
RED CROWN GAS STATION
at Simpson Avenue and 25th Street
in Hoquiam, Washington. Featuring
a free pit for crank case service.
Circa 1921.

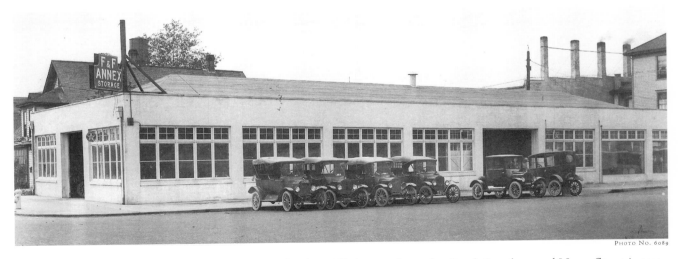

F & F ANNEX STORAGE AND FORD DEALERSHIP in Aberdeen, Washington located at South Broadway and Hume Street in 1921. Many years later it was H & H body repair shop until the building was about to fall down. It is now a recycle depot.

A RAILROAD SHIPMENT of 1922 Ford automobiles unloaded at the railroad freight terminal in Hoquiam, Washington. Eight vehicles minus fenders, bumpers, headlights and running boards (apparently all were optional equipment). They were all chained together and then towed by a tractor to Aberdeen Motors, three miles away. There, each vehicle was finished being assembled and made ready for the customers.

NORTH RIVER
TRANSPORTATION COMPANY'S
STRETCH LIMO in Aberdeen,
Washington to pick up
passengers. Circa 1924.

PACIFIC BEACH, Washington from an open cockpit biplane in 1924 featuring an Antique Car Club outing.

Quinault Lake General Merchandise,
Post Office and sidewalk gas pump for
tourists at this recreational area in Grays
Harbor County, Washington in 1925.

Photo No. 3399

Photo No. 4273

Tent Camping at
Joe Creek in Pacific Beach,
Washington, 1924. Probably
the county commissioners
had a sanitation problem.

M. M. Stewart Buick Agency at 412 East Market Street in Aberdeen, Washington. February 1925, showing the shop interior.

Peerless Service Station selling Union Oil Co. gasoline located on the south-west corner of Wishkah and K Streets in Aberdeen, Washington. Circa 1924. Building behind grease racks was parking garage for the Morck Hotel.

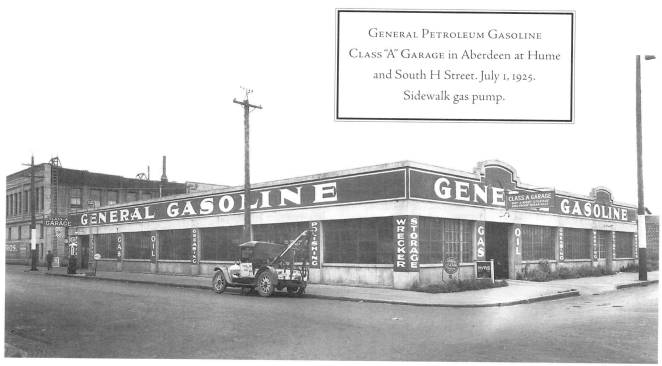

General Petroleum Gasoline Class "A" Garage in Aberdeen at Hume and South H Street. July 1, 1925. Sidewalk gas pump.

M. M. Stewart Buick Agency located at 412 East Market Street in Aberdeen, Washington. February 1925. Photo view of the shop interior.

ALEMITE SERVICE "SILVER
FLASH" RED CROWN GAS
STATION at Wishkah and K
Streets in Aberdeen,
Washington, 1926. In later
years it was called "City
Center Service". Photo taken
for Standard Oil Co.

M. M. STEWART BUICK AGENCY in Aberdeen, Washington located at 412 E. Market Street. A view of the shop interior,
February, 1925.

ABERDEEN BATTERY
COMPANY RED CROWN
GAS STATION located at
Wishkah and I Streets in
Aberdeen, featuring Fisk
Tires and Willard
Batteries. Photographed
in 1926.

PHOTO NO. 6131

PHOTO NO. 6157

MOTORCYCLE COP in front of the Aberdeen City Hall and Police Station with his Indian Scout twin-cylinder steed manufactured by Hendee Manufacturing Company of Springfield, Massachusetts. Photo taken circa 1920's.

RED CROWN GAS
STATION and Revie
Grease Racks in 1926.
Located in Hoquiam,
Washington at Fifth
and L Streets. Photo
taken for Standard
Oil Co.

PHOTO NO. 4540

PHOTO NO. 4537

RUSSELL'S RED CROWN GAS AND OIL SERVICE STATION and Cabin Tourist Park located in Aberdeen, Washington at Wishkah and Kansas Streets. Photo taken for Standard Oil Co. in 1926.

Charles Cyr Red Crown Gas Station located in Hoquiam, Washington at Simpson Avenue and 6th Street. Photo taken in 1926 for Standard Oil Co.

Standard Oil Co. of California Red Crown Gas Truck at the Standard Oil Company tank farm in Aberdeen, Washington. Circa 1926.

Harbor Oil Company, Distributors of General Petroleum Products tank farm and warehouse facilities at foot of Myrtle Street in Hoquiam, Washington. Circa 1927.

Photo No. 6144

Photo No. 6130

Stan DeLosh's Standard Oil Company Red Crown Gas Station in Aberdeen, Washington located at Wishkah and Broadway. Circa 1928.

ALBERT BENDETSON, a haberdasher owner with his new 1926 Buick 4 door sedan purchased from the M. M. Stewart Buick agency in Aberdeen, Washington. Photo taken in front of Mr. Bendetson's home on West fifth street in Aberdeen, November, 1926.

ELLISON MOTORS AUTHORIZED FORD SERVICE STATION featuring Red Crown Gas located in Hoquiam, Washington at Simpson Avenue and Ontario Street. Photo taken in 1926 for the Standard Oil Company.

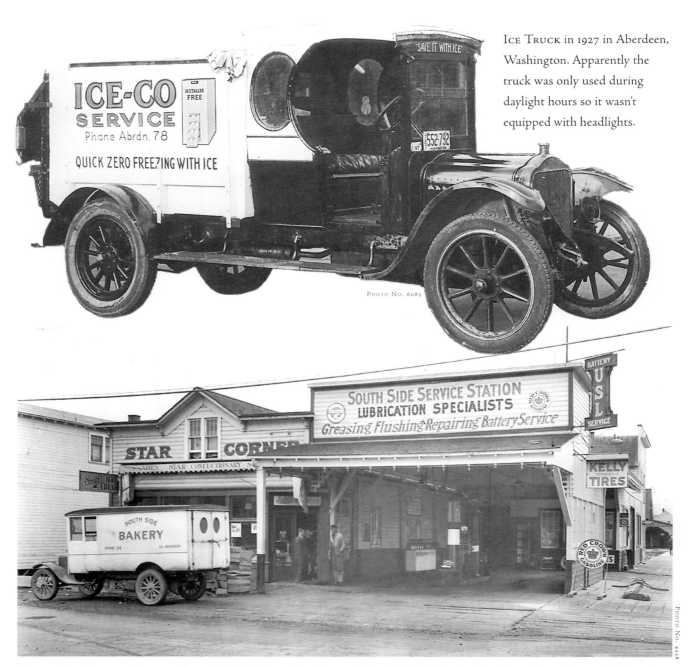

ICE TRUCK in 1927 in Aberdeen, Washington. Apparently the truck was only used during daylight hours so it wasn't equipped with headlights.

Photo No. 6085

Photo No. 4538

SOUTH SIDE SERVICE STATION featuring Red Crown Gasoline and Standard Oil Zerolene for Motor Cars. Located in Aberdeen, Washington at Star Corner of Curtis and Boone Streets in 1926.

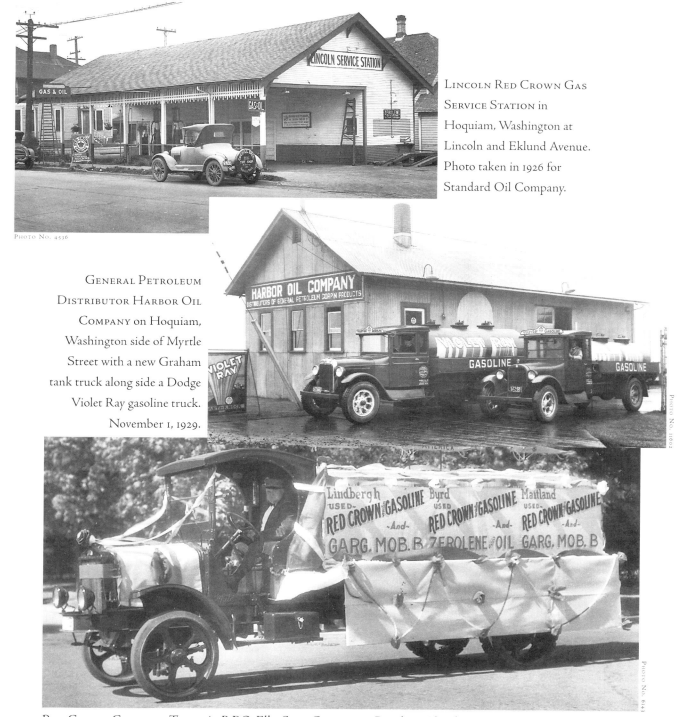

LINCOLN RED CROWN GAS SERVICE STATION in Hoquiam, Washington at Lincoln and Eklund Avenue. Photo taken in 1926 for Standard Oil Company.

GENERAL PETROLEUM DISTRIBUTOR HARBOR OIL COMPANY on Hoquiam, Washington side of Myrtle Street with a new Graham tank truck along side a Dodge Violet Ray gasoline truck. November 1, 1929.

RED CROWN GASOLINE TRUCK in B.P.O. Elks State Convention Parade in Aberdeen. June 1927. Signs on tank truck say Lindberg, Byrd and Maitland used Red Crown gas in their airplanes. Standard Oil Co. products.

RIGHT OUT OF THE ROARING 20's and the Keystone Cops was Bailey's Battery Patrol "Whippet" Paddy Wagon. Circa 1928. "If your battery gets Bad", call Bailey's. They will come with their bell clanging and a new Willard Battery to get you going.

PHOTO No. 6132

PHOTO No. 11503

PAY BOYD'S DIXIE SHELL STATION and baseball field. Sunday, August 4, 1929 from the roof of the dance pavilion showing the ball field and "Antique Car Collection". Brooklyn-North River area southwest of Cosmopolis, Washington.

North River Dixie Shell Service Baseball Park and Dance Pavilion near Brooklyn, Washington. Business owned by Pat Boyd, August 4, 1929. The community would gather at the dance hall every Saturday night then all would stay for a baseball game on Sunday.

Bob Isaacson's Grays Harbor Equipment Co. Model "T" Ford in 1928 headed to the logging camps in the northwest forest country. This firm is still the same family business in 1998. Located in Aberdeen. Note the white sidewall tires.

Photo No. 6009

INTER-CITY SERVICE STATION selling General Petroleum Violet Ray Gasoline. Located at Simpson Avenue and 28th Street in Hoquiam, Washington. May 7, 1929.

DOCTOR CHAMBERLAIN taking delivery of his new 1928 Model "A" Ford sport business coupe from Lee Bigelow in Aberdeen, Washington. A 1906 Model "N" Ford which today would be worth a fortune, was incorporated in the photo to give some contrast between the old and the new. Even the 1928 model would be worth far more than the $525.00 original price.

RIVERSIDE PARK near New London on U. S. 101 outside of Hoquiam, Washington. Specializing in Red Crown Gasoline. The author learned to drive in the 1923 Maxwell Coach that is fueling up. March 14, 1929.

MONTESANO AUTO CO. Red Crown Gas Station with curbside pumps in Montesano, Washington, 1926. Ford Authorized Service Shop.

ABERDEEN MOTORS, located at Market and L Streets in Aberdeen with 1926 new Fords. It was managed by Lee Bigelow for the Titus family who had other dealerships in three other cities. After the stockmarket crash in 1929, the bank took over the business and had Lee Bigelow operate it and eventually Bigelow became the owner.

EARL HUNT's Richfield two canopy service
station at Broadway and Market streets in
downtown Aberdeen, with Reid Brothers
Richfield gas and oil trucks. The photo was
taken for the Braley Motor Company dealers for
Dodge Brothers and Graham Brothers Trucks.

PHOTO NO. 11603

PHOTO NO. 11376

LES THOMPSON DESOTO AGENCY in Aberdeen on Broadway featuring the 1929 vehicles. *Left to Right:* Sedan Coach, $1194.00;
Roadster Especial $1050.00; 4-Door Sedan $1160.00 and another Roadster $1174.00. DeSoto delivered a total of 81,065 cars in
1929, a first year sales achievement that lasted for thirty years. Photo taken May 7, 1929.

1923 MAXWELL two door coach with author Bill and sister Helen in 1929 when their father bought the used car from the M. M. Stewart Buick Dealer in Aberdeen. Bill learned to drive this vehicle between 10 and 11 years old.

A RICHFIELD FAIRWAY SERVICE STATION under construction May 15, 1929 at Wishkah and So. Newell Streets. The roofing material was Western Red Cedar Tile manufactured by Victor H. Street.

The Motoring 30s

TEXACO SERVICE STATION at Simpson and 9th Street in Hoquiam, February 3, 1931, about the time of its grand opening. The architecture of this structure appears that it was probably designed in Southern California with a Spanish tinge of stucco. Not really a good exterior in the Northwest rain country.

PHOTO NO. 12182

TEXACO GASOLINE AND MOTOR OIL STATION in Hoquiam—a year and a half after opening at Simpson Avenue and 9th Street. The shrubbery has grown and the service department is thriving. Photo taken July 27, 1932 with camera and tripod from a platform on the roof of the photographer's automobile.

PHOTO NO. 12819

PHOTO NO. 12059

JAMESON'S GROCERY AND RED CROWN GAS plus Seaboard Gasoline on South Boone Street in Aberdeen. November 1, 1930.

LESLIE PETROLEUM COMPANY'S Hoh Oil Well prospecting for oil December 2, 1931 near the Hoh River on the Quinault Indian Reservation in the State of Washington and the Pacific Ocean. Rumors were that they struck oil of high enough grade that it was poured into the gas tank of a model "T" Ford and driven away. A number of bottles of the oil were distributed to various people to publicize the find. The photographer and author still has a quart bottle.

PHOTO NO. 12588

PACIFIC BEACH,
WASHINGTON on
Sunday, July 26, 1931,
features a Shell
curbside gas pump
and farther down the
block two additional
pumps, one on each
side of the street.

BRALEY MOTORS with shipment of four new 1930 Nash Automobiles. Note a single axle at the rear of the trailer and a single axle on the truck. Also, the bridge construction of the long flat bed trailer. A far cry from the convoy trailers they use to deliver new vehicles to the dealer today. Photo taken July 2, 1930 with an 8x10" view camera and tripod.

BYE THOMPSON'S COPALIS BEACH SEASHORE CAMP with two Shell Oil Co. ten-gallon hand operated pumps. A 1923 Maxwell two door sedan is fueling up. Photo taken July 1931, Copalis Beach, Grays Harbor County, Washington.

ANOTHER PHOTO OF BYE THOMPSON'S Copalis Beach Resort on State Highway 109, taken in July of 1933. The big beach umbrella over two 10 gallon cylinder pumps refueled the tourists. Here a 1927 Chrysler owned by the photographer was getting gassed.

STAN DELOSH's Standard Oil Co. Station at Broadway and Wishkah Streets in Aberdeen, Washington on April 28, 1931. Featuring U. S. Royal Cord tires, Standard Ethyl Gasoline, Willard Batteries, Hyvis Motor Oil and *personalized service.*

PHOTO No. 12285

PHOTO No. 11602

QUEETS INN AND SHELL OIL DEALER on Quinault Indian Reservation. Queets, Washington, August 28, 1931. Photographer and author stayed at this hotel when the Olympic Highway Loop U.S. 101 opened. The 9-year-old author's family drove there in a 1923 Maxwell two door sedan.

MOTOR VILLAGE AT PACIFIC BEACH, Washington shows eleven of the 24 individual units with a garage for each auto, the forerunner of the motel where you did your own "bellhopping". February 25, 1931.

PHOTO No. 11602

MOTOR VILLAGE AUTO COURT AND SERVICE STATION furnishing Mobil and Zerolene Oil at Pacific Beach, Washington. There were 24 individual units with carport for each cabin. This was the forerunner of the modern motel, but today your automobile is parked in a parking lot exposed to the weather. February 25, 1931.

PHOTO No. 12208-C

PHOTO No. 12533

SHELL LOG CABIN CAMP with four units in Central Park on State Highway 12, six miles east of Aberdeen. Cars were parked out of the weather, next to each cabin. September 24, 1931.

MOIR'S ASSOCIATED GAS STATION at Simpson Avenue and Ninth Street in Hoquiam, March 1, 1930.

FRED HALBERT'S AUTO TOURIST CAMP at Lake Quinault in the Olympic National Park, May 25, 1930. Each cabin had a shelter for the car. The lady could get a glass of cold water from the single outside faucet, and for heat there was a double-bit axe and firewood to split. The author learned to row a boat at this campground.

U. S. Royal Rubber Co. requested a photograph of Stan DeLosh's Red Crown Service Station, January 11, 1930. Located at Wishkah and Broadway. It was one of the largest and most popular stations in the city of Aberdeen for U. S. Royal Cord Tires, Willard Batteries and Standard Oil Co. products.

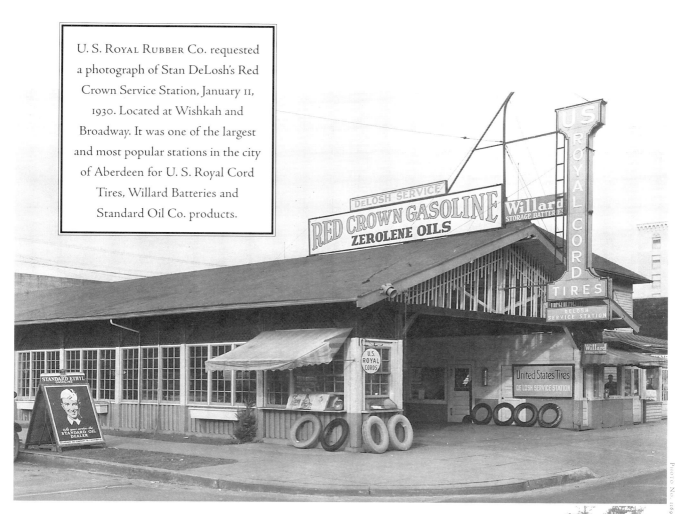

Becker's Kalaloch Resort at Kalaloch, Washington on U.S. 101, for the Olympic Highway Loop opening celebration. The ribbon was cut at the Kalaloch River Bridge on August 28, 1931. The station was a Standard Oil Co. dealer.

COPALIS MERCANTILE
AND RICHFIELD VIOLET
RAY GAS, L. F. BERRY,
Proprietor, located at
Copalis Beach, Washington
on State Highway 109.
Photograph taken in 1931 by
Bliss B. Jones.

A. B. GRIFFITH'S HARBOR VIEW RICHFIELD SERVICE STATION on U. S. Highway 12 just east of the city limits of Aberdeen.
Photograph taken on February 3, 1931.

RICHFIELD FAIRWAY SERVICE STATION at East Wishkah and South Newell Streets. July 19, 1932.

TEXACO TANK TRUCK delivering petroleum products to the Wilson Bros. sawmill in Aberdeen. June 25, 1930.

STUDEBAKER 8 COMMANDER REGAL SEDAN displayed by Craft Motor Company at the Ice Palace located at Simpson and Park Streets in Aberdeen, Washington. Photograph taken in June of 1930.

STANDARD OIL STATION and Auto Camp at 701 East Wishkah and Kansas Streets. Originally Russell's Red Crown Gas and Cabin Camp. Photo taken July 19, 1932.

PHOTO NO. 12805

PHOTO NO. 13335

SUNSET OAKLAND COMPANY, dealers in Hudson-Essex-Terraplane automobiles in Aberdeen at 521 East First Street. The NRA signs in the window indicates it was the big depression years of March 15, 1934.

PHOTO NO. 13933

SCHALLIAR'S GENERAL PETROLEUM CORP. FLYING RED HORSE PROMOTION of the new General 4 Star Gasoline with the help of the American Legion Drum and Bugle Corp. May 23, 1933 at Wishkah and L Streets in Aberdeen. Socony Certified Lubrication Service.

AL LAWRENCE'S General Petroleum Service Station located at 9th and J Street in Hoquiam, with the American Legion Drum and Bugle Corp. celebrating a Flying Red Horse Promotion. The rain couldn't dampen the enthusiasm on May 23, 1933.

AL LAWRENCE'S SERVICE STATION. The spare tire cover advertises Violet Ray Gas Anti-knock. The Flying Red Horse was promoting the New General 4 Star Gasoline.

RAY McGOWAN's Flying Red Horse Mobilgas Station in Aberdeen at Wishkah and L Streets. Two islands with two 10 gallon cylinder pumps each and full service attendants. February 7, 1936.

JOE SPENCER IN ABERDEEN in October 1934 when severe winter storms and high tides flooded the downtown streets. Joe had an auto repair shop located in the 100 block of West Market Street, and got out his 1902 Buick or possibly and Auburn. According to a book on vintage automobiles, the Buick didn't arrive until 1904, yet there is a Buick emblem just above the white sign. The Auburn automobile was in existence in 1902.

PLANK ROAD in the Hoh Indian Reservation on the coast. Taken for the Hoh River Oil Company, April 6, 1934.

GENERAL PETROLEUM Flying Red Horse Mobilgas Station owned by Ray McGowan at Wishkah and L Streets in Aberdeen, featuring Certified Mobilubrication Service, U. S. Royal Tires and Bear Wheel Alignment. February 7, 1936.

GOODYEAR SERVICE STATION and Tire Store in Aberdeen, located at Wishkah and Jefferson Streets, with service personnel in front. May 20, 1935.

GILMORE RED LION GAS STATION at the corner of Wishkah and Jefferson Streets in Aberdeen, July 1934. Botsford, Constatine and Gardner had the photograph taken.

RICHFIELD OIL CO. AND DISTRIBUTION CENTER located at 805 East Wishkah and South Harbor Streets in Aberdeen. The Service Station was constructed with Super Harbord Plywood manufactured by Harbor Plywood Corp. of Aberdeen and Hoquiam.

PEERLESS MOBILGAS
SERVICE STATION located
at Wishkah and K Streets
in Aberdeen, promoting
Flying Red Horse
Mobilgas service.
March 19, 1937.

ASSOCIATED DRIVE-THROUGH SERVICE STATION located at Heron and K Streets in Aberdeen, 1935. This was the location of the very
first Service Station in Aberdeen in 1917. It was so successful the owner, Lee Bigelow wanted to open one in Hoquiam, about 4 miles
away. However, the bank in Seattle turned down the loan and said that one service station in the county was enough.

Ted Schwarz Union Oil Station opening night in Aberdeen, August 8, 1935. Two search lights put a finishing touch of a Hollywood Production at Wishkah and I Streets.

Ted Schwarz Union 76 Gas Station in Aberdeen, May 22, 1959. 29 years after opening, the station was torn down to make way for a modern Minute Man 76 structure, but Ted remained open to take care of his customers who needed gasoline.

Ted Schwarz' New Minute Man Union 76 Service Station on the same site that originally opened in 1935 in Aberdeen.

GENERAL PETROLEUM
WAKEFIELD MOTORS
MOBILGAS STATION
located at Market and L
Streets in Aberdeen.
Wakefield was also the
Ford Dealer Agency across
Market Street from the gas
station. July 21, 1937.

JENSEN'S SHELL SERVICE STATION with some of the uniformed attendants in Aberdeen at Wishkah and Park Streets on U. S. 101 in July 1937.

A STREET SCENE in Aberdeen in June 1936, during the heart of the Great Depression. Still, there were some 1935 and 1936 vehicles among the many older vehicles. Photo taken from a platform on top of a 1935 Plymouth.

B.F. GOODRICH SILVERTOWN STORE in Aberdeen. Originally, it was a General Petroleum Violet Ray Gas Station owned by Fred Hood and was located at First and Broadway until 1937. Fred was sent to Grays Harbor by Packard Motor Co. as a specialist in servicing their automobiles. Because of the high percentage of Packard owners among the lumber and logging families in the area, Packard wanted their cars serviced right. B. F. Goodrich Silvertown took over the Fred Hood Station in the late 1930s. This photograph was taken August 15, 1939.

Day Motor Co., Standard Oil Products and Ford Dealer in Elma, Washington, March 12, 1938. For a small town, this facility was very impressive and many vehicles were sold from Day.

MobilOil Dodge and Plymouth Factory Approved Lube Rack at Braley Motors Dodge and Plymouth Dealership in Aberdeen. August 26, 1937.

WARREN BROS. SIGNAL STATION nearing completion in Aberdeen, on East Wishkah Street. Constructed of Super-Harbord weatherproof plywood which was manufactured by Harbor Plywood Corp. of Aberdeen and Hoquiam. June 23, 1938.

WARREN BROS. SIGNAL SERVICE STATION Grand Opening, July 7, 1938.

GENERAL PETROLEUM
MOBILGAS and Hoquiam
Ford Motors East Side
Branch at Simpson Ave. and
Ontario with a 1937 Ford
Sedan parked outside the
show window. The black
smoke was probably from the
Polson's Eureka sawmill or
Grays Harbor Pulp and
Paper Mill. July 20, 1937.

STANDARD OIL CO. STATIONS, INC. located
at Milwaukee Avenue and Powell Blvd in
Portland, Oregon. The building was
constructed of Super-Harbord Plywood
which was made by Harbor Plywood Corp.
in Hoquiam. October 15, 1939.

JENSEN'S SHELL
SERVICE STATION at
Wishkah and Park
Streets in Aberdeen
on U.S. 101. July 1937.

SOUTHWORTH'S SUPER SERVICE featuring Washington Chief Gasoline from six pumps on two islands. This station was located at Park and Market Streets in Aberdeen and was also constructed of Super Harbord Plywood. Photo taken for Harbor Plywood Corp. on December 27, 1939.

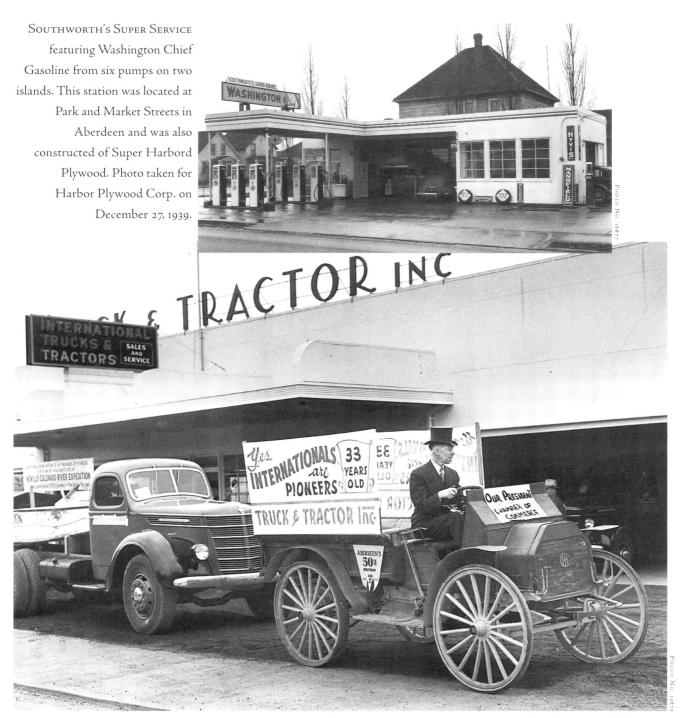

TRUCK & TRACTOR INTERNATIONAL TRUCK DEALER in Aberdeen, with the owner A. George Sutcliff at the wheel of a 1905 International truck. Photo taken August 27, 1938 with a new '38 model International truck behind.

Super Harbord Plywood

and the stations it built...

PHOTO NO. 11602

MOBILGAS SERVICE STATION under construction at 33rd and Division Streets in Portland, Oregon on May 13, 1939. Another station constructed with Super Harbord Plywood.

THE FINISHED STATION, on October 15, 1939. Photograph taken for Harbor Plywood Corp.

PHOTO NO. 16768

Standard Oil Co. Station at 52nd and Division Streets in Portland, Oregon. October 15, 1939.

Photo No. 11602

Standard Stations, Inc. new station in Forest Grove, Oregon. October 15, 1939.

Photo No. 16767

Art's Maywood Service featuring Union Oil Products at 92nd and Prescot in Portland, Oregon. Photo taken December 31, 1939 for Harbor Plywood Corp.

SHELL OIL CO. SERVICE
STATION in Portland, Oregon.
Built of Super Harbord
Plywood. May 13, 1939.

STANDARD OIL CO. authorized distributor in this "Log" Service Station located at Heron and Chehalis Streets in Aberdeen. This photo shows the owner as John Niemi, June 17, 1939. It was probably built about 1933 and operated as Frontier Service Station by Gunner Rath until 1936. James Eubanks operated it 1937–38. Red Patton had it in 1940, Art Brueher in 1941 and M.W. Canfield in August 1945. How many owners in between is anybody's guess.

BECKER'S KALALOCH
RESORT on U. S. 101 at
Kalaloch, Washington.
Standard Oil Co. dealer,
July 9, 1939.

MOBIL FLYING RED HORSE SERVICE
STATION in Portland, Oregon on
May 13, 1939. Station constructed of
Super-Harbord Plywood.

MOBILGAS FLYING RED HORSE
STATION constructed with Super-
Harbord Plywood. This station
was located in Portland, Oregon.
May 13, 1939.

A BRAND NEW SERVICE STATION at Market and Park Streets constructed with Super Harbord Plywood. November 27, 1939.

SOUTHWORTH'S SUPER WASHINGTON CHIEF gas station in Aberdeen. December 27, 1939.

CENTRAL PARK TEXACO photographed January 20, 1938. Central Park, Washington is about five miles east of Aberdeen on U. S. Hwy 12 which starts in Aberdeen and goes to Chicago, Illinois.

PHOTO No. 15387

PHOTO No. 16766

STANDARD OIL CO. STATION at 82nd and Division Streets in Portland, Oregon. Built of Super-Harbord Plywood. October 15, 1939.

ART CARSON'S SHELL STATION located on John Richardson Road in Hoquiam. With four ten-gallon cylinder pumps and tire service recapping and vulcanizing specialists.

PHOTO No. 16939

O'NEIL'S GENERAL MERCHANDISE Post Office and Shell gasoline pump in the beach community of Tokeland located in Willapa Harbor, Pacific County, Washington. Circa 1940.

WICKMAN'S MOBILGAS STATION located at Randall and "B" Streets in Aberdeen, Washington, November 7, 1939. This station had several different partners and owners over a period of more than 50 years distributing Mobil and Standard Oil products at different times.

Photo No. 16794

STANDARD OIL CO. STATION operated by Leo Kosenski at Simpson Ave. and 28th Street in Hoquiam, Washington, June 17, 1939.

Photo No. 16469

The Victorious 40s

Union Oil Dealer in new Super-Harbord Plywood station located in St. Helens, Oregon. March 13, 1940.

Photo No. 17064

Photo No. 16467

Morehead Bros. Standard Oil Dealer at 1st and "G" Streets in Aberdeen, Washington. June 17, 1939.

AMBULANCES at Hoquiam General Hospital on
Sixth and K Streets. July 1940.

HAGENAH'S GARAGE AND UNION OIL DEALER at
85th and Powell Blvd. in Portland, Oregon. Station
constructed with Super-Harbor Plywood.

GAIL REED'S "HAPPY LANDING" SHELL OIL CO. STATION located at 148th and Stark in Portland, Oregon. Station built with
Super-Harbor Plywood. Photograph taken March 13, 1940.

General Petroleum's Mobilgas Station managed by Lougheed and Shorey in Montesano, Washington. This station was also built with Super-Harbord Plywood. September 28, 1940.

Hugh Bailey Automotive Service and Parts Store in Aberdeen at 111 North Broadway. Another building made of Super-Harbord Plywood. July 19, 1940.

Flying Red Horse Dress being modeled by Mrs. Martha Frederickson at the George J. Wolff Store in Aberdeen. The Ad read "General's Symbol of Quality Finds Its Way Into the Fashion Shops of Wolff's, Flying Horse Printed Afternoon Dress, $16.95." April 12, 1940.

Left: Fabric detail

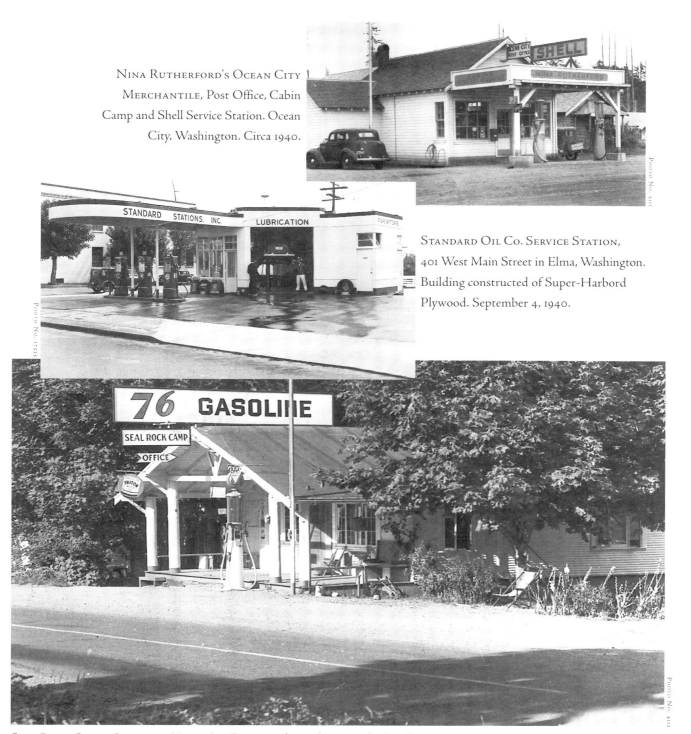

Nina Rutherford's Ocean City Mercantile, Post Office, Cabin Camp and Shell Service Station. Ocean City, Washington. Circa 1940.

Standard Oil Co. Service Station, 401 West Main Street in Elma, Washington. Building constructed of Super-Harbord Plywood. September 4, 1940.

Seal Rock Cabin Camp and Union '76 Gasoline located on Hood's Canal, U. S. 101 near Brinnon, Washington, Olympic Peninsula.

TWENTY-FIFTH ANNIVERSARY model Hudson Super 6 at The Sunset Co. in Aberdeen. The New Hudson Drive Master, no clutch pushing and no gear shifting with a 102 horsepower engine. Cleve Jackson is the proud new owner. October 15, 1941.

PHOTO NO. 18761

PHOTO NO. 17588

TWO SERVICE STATIONS across from each other at Chehalis and Heron Street in Aberdeen. September 21, 1940. A Standard Oil Co. Distributor "Red" Patton and across the street was Pacific Service Station featuring MobilGas and Mobil Oil products. Gunnar Rath operated both stations at the same time. The log structure as Frontier Service selling Richfield products from 1933 to 1936. The Pacific Service was operated by Rath from 1926 to 1946.

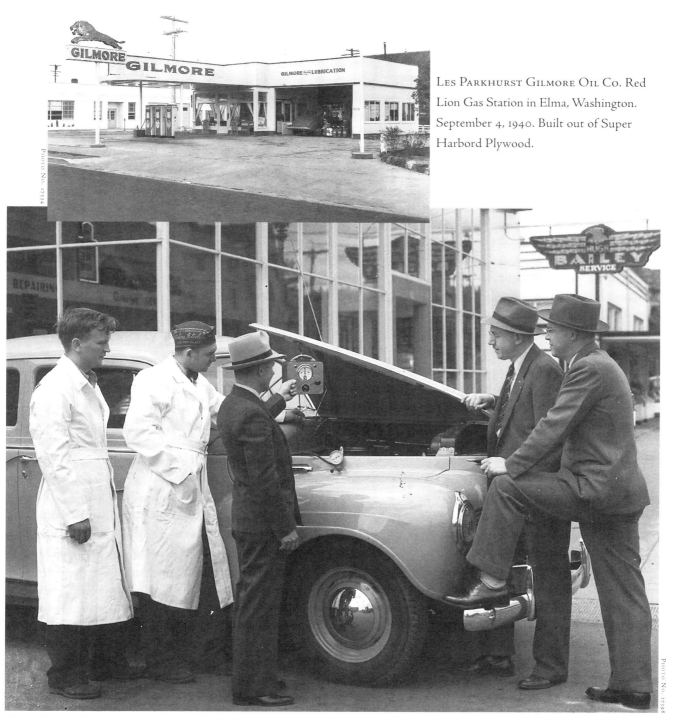

LES PARKHURST GILMORE OIL CO. Red Lion Gas Station in Elma, Washington. September 4, 1940. Built out of Super Harbord Plywood.

HUGH BAILEY SERVICE in Aberdeen, demonstrating a new diagnostic testing instrument for automobile engines. July 15, 1940.

ASSOCIATED FLYING "A" SERVICE STATION destroyed by fire in Elma, Washington at 6th and Main Street. Photograph taken September 4, 1940 for Harbor Plywood Corp.

PHOTO NO. 17533

NEW ASSOCIATED FLYING "A" SERVICE STATION built with Super-Harbord weatherproof plywood to replace the metal station that was destroyed by fire earlier in the year. Located at Sixth and Main Street in Elma, Washington.

PHOTO NO. 17759

PHOTO NO. 18434

MOBILOIL NEW ABERDEEN GARAGE and Western Auto Supply Co. at Broadway and Market Streets in Aberdeen. JUNE 24, 1941.

SHELL OIL CO. NEW STATION c-929 located at 8th and Simpson Avenue in Hoquiam in 1941.

PHOTO NO. 19482

PHOTO NO. 18796

GENERAL TIRE SERVICE AND HANCOCK GASOLINE at Wishkah and M Street in Aberdeen. Specializing in recapping your old tires with new treads. October 25, 1941.

OLYMPIC MOTORS, INC.
DeSoto Plymouth
Dealer Robert W. Bryne
located at Market and K
Street in Aberdeen.
January 27, 1941. DeSoto
Fluid Drive Transmission.
Bryne was also a dealer for
Diamond T Trucks.

GENERAL TIRE SERVICE at Wishkah and M Streets in Aberdeen. Interior of the retreading plant where they gave new life to your tires. Photo taken October 25, 1941.

Truck and Tractor, Inc. Chrysler & Plymouth and International Truck Dealers in Aberdeen. Carl Hahn (left) the former dealer of Chrysler and Plymouth congratulates A. George Sutcliff on the grand opening of the new 1941 Chrysler products dealership. February 24, 1941.

Photo No. 18068

GOODYEAR TIRES AND GAS STATION in Aberdeen, Washington located at Wishkah and Jefferson Streets. August 1942.

PHOTO NO. 19733

The author, WILLIAM D. JONES with his first automobile, a 1930 Chevrolet Coupe with 6 cylinder engine. It was purchased used for $75.00. The first thing after purchasing it was that father insisted that the car get new brakes. He said that if it wouldn't run that was okay but if it wouldn't stop that wasn't okay. It was driven for a little over a year and on the day of this photograph, November 15, 1941. It was traded in for $50.00 on a 1933 Plymouth 4 door sedan which had hydraulic brakes and an all steel body for $225.00.

GENERAL PETROLEUM FLYING RED HORSE SIGN made of Super-Harbord weatherproof plywood. This sign being displayed by Mr. M. S. Munson, Sales Manager of Harbor Plywood Corp. The sign had been in use for several years exposed to all the elements of weather and was still in good condition.

Photo No. 19027

Photo No. 18770

ED LAFFERTY MOBILGAS STATION in Montesano, Washington located at Sylvia and Pioneer Avenue. This photograph was used in an advertisement in the Montesano *Vidette* on November 6, 1941, one month before the Pearl Harbor Day of Infamy.

ENGEN'S UNION '76 SERVICE STATION and Ford
Agency in Montesano, Washington located at
301 Pioneer Avenue East.

WHITNEY'S brought out a
Buick-Chevrolet and GMC
Dealership in 1922 and the
business is still operating on
the same corner in
Montesano, Washington
selling Shell gasoline and
Oldsmobile-Chevrolet and
GMC Trucks. Another big
business in a small town.
Taken July 30, 1942.

EMERY GRIFFITH'S ASSOCIATED
STATION selling Flying "A" Gas,
located at Wishkah and F Street
in Aberdeen. January 14, 1941.

Bigelow Chevrolet Co. at Market and L Streets exterior with the banner advertising the unveiling of the new 1942 Chevrolets in Aberdeen. Photo taken September 27, 1941.

Bigelow Chevrolet Co. unveiling the new 1942 Chevrolet automobiles at Market and L Streets in Aberdeen. September 27, 1941, ten weeks before Pearl Harbor. Interior of the sales room.

PHOTO NO. 22458-C

STANDARD OIL CO. DEALER Beachway Service at 200 W. Emerson Avenue in Hoquiam. Photo taken June 1946.

STANDARD OIL CO. DEALER Picco Motors located in Montesano at 126 East Pioneer Avenue. Studebaker Dealer and Chevron Gas photograph taken June 1946.

PHOTO NO. 22458-B

PHOTO NO. 23168

THE SUNSET CO. HUDSON AUTOMOBILE DEALER Ransom Minkler at 521 East First Street in Aberdeen. January 1947.

ARCTIC SERVICE STATION—Standard Oil Products on Highway U. S. 101 between Aberdeen and Raymond, Washington. The Red and White Stores for groceries and confection. Photo taken August 23, 1945.

Joe Koski's Richfield Station and Cabin Camp located at Wishkah and Alder Streets in Aberdeen, Washington. April 25, 1944 during World War II.

White City Standard Oil Products Dealer and Cabin Camp on U. S. Highway 12 about four miles east of Aberdeen. Also had facilities for travel trailers. June 1946.

Sylvester T. "Buck" Bodey (center) having survived the Battle of the Bulge and four other battles as an ambulance driver with Patton's army during World War II, takes delivery of the first post-war Ford to reach Aberdeen and Ruddach & Morehead Ford Dealership. Photo taken December 8, 1945.

Mobilgas Flying Red Horse Station located in Portland, Oregon. Photo taken May 13, 1939.

Photo No. 16190

Photo No. 21007

Official United States Government Tire Inspection Station at the Firestone store in Aberdeen during World War II. July 1, 1944. Located at Wishkah and M Streets.

AL BERTHOLD MOTORS DESOTO & PLYMOUTH dealership in Hoquiam, April 4, 1946. This was the first shipment on new cars after World War II.

PHOTO NO. 22285

PHOTO NO. 22458-D

STANDARD OIL DEALER Rowe and Williams located at 220 Lincoln Street in Hoquiam, June 1946.

1946 CHRYSLER with Fluid Drive Transmission in the showroom of the Allen Brother's Chrysler & Plymouth and Chevron gas dealer garage located in Silverton, Oregon. One of the first vehicles manufactured after World War II.

SIMON KRETZ combination service station and residence at 374 Queen Avenue in Hoquiam, Washington. June 1946.

Standard Oil Co. Dealer M. W. Canfield, located at Chehalis and Heron Streets, Aberdeen. August 23, 1945.

Photo No. 21946

Photo No. 22482

Allen Bros. Chrysler & Plymouth Automobiles and Allis Chalmers Farm Equipment and Chevron Gasoline. The business was established in 1923 in Silverton, Oregon. The Brother's parents crossed the plains in covered wagons from Illinois to Oregon in 1852 on the Oregon Trail. The author's great-grandmother was a member of the Allen Family. Photo taken in 1946.

A RAILROAD BOX CAR SHIPMENT of 1941 Packards for the Atlas Motors Dealership in Aberdeen. Two of the vehicles were suspended from the ceiling of the railroad car while others were parked underneath and anchored to the floor.

STANDARD OIL CO. MOREHEAD BROS. Station after being remodeled at First and G Streets in Aberdeen. November 28, 1945.

STANDARD OIL CO. CHEVRON Station in Aberdeen at Heron and K Streets. January 27, 1946.

Packard Motor Cars and Chevron gasoline products at Atlas Motors in Aberdeen at Heron and K Streets. Service Department. February 20, 1948.

Atlas Motors Packard Agency and Chevron products located at Heron and K Streets in Aberdeen, Washington. The owner was requested by Packard to send in some photographs of his dealership. He hired a photographer to do the job, but after seeing the photos he knew he would lose his agency. He then hired us to do the photography. We told him the first thing that he'd better clean up the place and paint the floor, which he did. We then set up the 8x10 view camera on a tripod right at dusk when the light intensity on the outside was the same as the artificial light on the inside. He was thrilled with the results and managed to retain his dealership of Packards. February 20, 1948.

RUNDELL MOTORS AND NASH DEALER, located at Market and M Streets in Aberdeen. January 29, 1948.

RUNDELL MOTORS AND NASH
AUTOMOBILE DEALER. Maintenance shop
interior taken January 29, 1948.

CHEVRON STATION
OPENING with Ray
Neinast, Proprietor
at Market and H Streets
in Aberdeen.
March 5, 1948.

RAY NEINAST Chevron Station opening with Standard Oil Co. and city officials, March 5, 1948.

Ray Neinast Chevron station lube bay on opening day.

Ray Neinast Chevron station on opening day.

CHET NELSON'S STATION pumping "Aviation Brand" gas at Market and Park Streets in Aberdeen, Washington. Photo taken for Shell Oil Company. June 14, 1948.

A NEW CHEVRON SERVICE STATION located at Broadway and State Street in Aberdeen, waiting for new signs and a grand opening. February, 1947.

MOBILGAS AND HUDSON DEALER at Glenn Motors in Satsop, Washington. September, 1948.

LEE'S SERVICE AND CABINS—a Time oil station located at Wishkah and Alder under new management, July 25, 1947.

TRUCK AND TRACTOR CHRYSLER, PLYMOUTH & INTERNATIONAL TRUCK DEALERSHIP in Aberdeen on Simpson Ave. and Scammel Street. October, 1948.

PHOTO NO. 24918

INTERIOR OF HUFFMAN MOTORS LINCOLN MERCURY dealership showroom and parts counter in Aberdeen, located at First and I Streets. April 30, 1949.

PHOTO NO. 24916

HUFFMAN MOTORS, LINCOLN MERCURY DEALERSHIP in Aberdeen at First and I Streets. Owned by "Cowboy" Carl Huffman in his new building April 30, 1949.

The Rockin' 50s

LOUDIN MOBILGAS STATION and Kaiser Frazer Agency at 821 J Street in Hoquiam. Flying Red Horse Gas, and note the Crosley pick-up at the pump. Taken July 1947.

PHOTO NO. 23673

TEXACO GAS PUMPS at the Firestone Service Center in Aberdeen at Wishkah and M Street. April 29, 1950. Fire Chief and Sky Chief gasoline. The rubber hose on the floor would activate at bell when a vehicle drove over it and an attendant would appear to give you service.

General Tire Service Bay for installing retreaded tires on vehicles. Aberdeen, November 9, 1951.

General Tire Service, located at Wishkah and M Streets after remodeling. July 3, 1951.

General Tire Service retreaded the old worn out tires if the carcass was not rotten and the sidewalls of the tire were in good shape. November 9, 1951.

Texaco and Havoline Motor Oils in the Lube Department of the Firestone Service Center in Aberdeen at Wishkah and M Street. April 29, 1950.

Joe Ramsey Motor's Employees in Aberdeen unload an automobile railroad box car shipment of four Kaiser and/or Frazer sedans. Two vehicles were suspended from the roof of the box car while two others were secured underneath the hanging ones. June 1950.

WHITNEY OLDSMOBILE DEALERSHIP in Aberdeen at Broadway and Market Street. October 31, 1951.

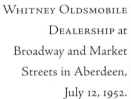

WHITNEY OLDS and General Tire Service in Aberdeen. Located at Market and Broadway. Photograph taken on November 6, 1951.

WHITNEY OLDSMOBILE DEALERSHIP at Broadway and Market Streets in Aberdeen, July 12, 1952.

LLOYD HALL'S MOBILE GAS STATION in Elma, Washington

LLOYD HALL'S MOBILE GAS STATION in Elma, Washington at Second and Main Street. April 6, 1953. Lloyd's wife Jean presents a tide book to a customer for a fill-up of Mobil gas in his 1948 Dodge 4 door sedan.

U. S. Royal and Earley Tire Co. at Wishkah and Park Streets in Aberdeen. Owned by John Earley who became President of National Tire Dealers Association. Photo taken June 16, 1953.

S & F Mobil Station, 301 West Wishkah Street, Aberdeen. April 15, 1953.

MobilGas Flying Red Horse Station operated by Bob Lantz at Lincoln and 5th Streets in Hoquiam, April 2, 1953.

S & F Mobil Station, Ed Stultz and Will Flaherty. Grand opening April 15, 1953.

S & W Tire Service, Firestone Tires and Texaco gasoline grand opening celebration. Aberdeen, at Wishkah and M Streets owned by George W. Smith and V. I. Whitney. November 11, 1953.

S & W Tire Service grand opening "Guess the weight of the tire" contest. Firestone tires and Texaco gasoline.

A U. S. Navy Chief takes possession of a new Nash Rambler from dealer Jack Rundell of Rundell Motors in Aberdeen. July 1, 1953.

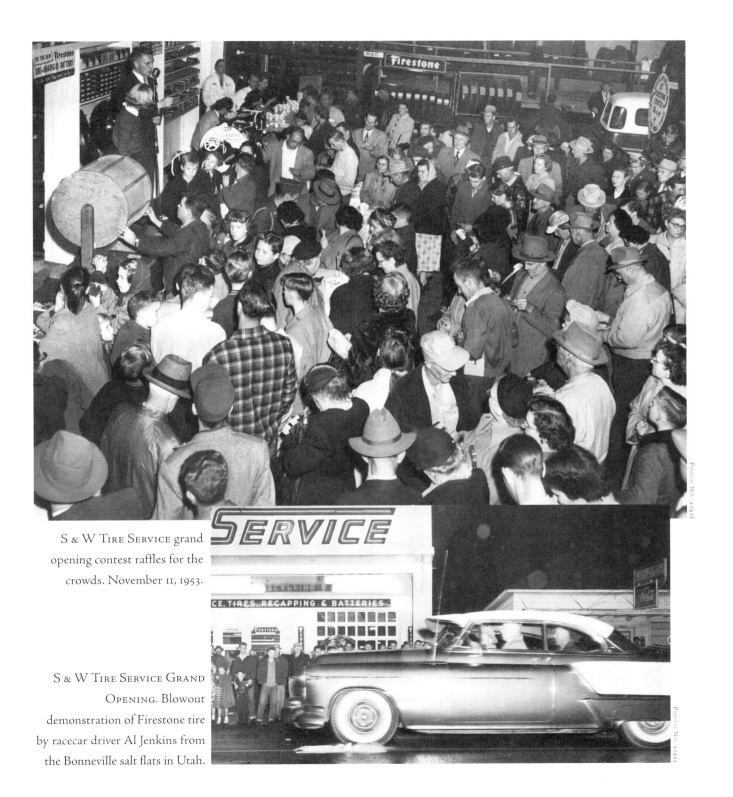

S & W Tire Service grand opening contest raffles for the crowds. November 11, 1953.

S & W Tire Service Grand Opening. Blowout demonstration of Firestone tire by racecar driver Al Jenkins from the Bonneville salt flats in Utah.

SHELL EDGEWORTH SERVICE STATION damaged by a runaway trailer that knocked down a gas pump and the canopy which required the fire department from Aberdeen to hose down the spilled gasoline. The station was located about three miles east of Aberdeen on U. S. Highway 12. November 15, 1954.

Earley Tire Co. and U. S. Royal Tire dealer at Wishkah and Park Streets in Aberdeen. April 1954.

General Petroleum Corp. Mobil Junior Safety Economy Run for Elma High School students. Hall's Mobil Station, May 14, 1955. Each vehicle is filled with gas and then the tank cap sealed. All drivers travel the same course and distance and then return to Hall's Mobil where the seal is broken and the tank refilled to determine who travelled the course using the least amount of fuel.

Bob Dotson's brand new Texaco Service Station at Simpson Ave. and Haight Street in Aberdeen. November 1, 1955, filling the tank with Sky Chief gasoline.

Bob Dotson Texaco
Service Station
at Simpson and Haight
Streets in Aberdeen.
November 1, 1955.

1902 OLDSMOBILE
on tour to
Aberdeen,
August 8, 1958.

PHOTO NO. 33404

GENERAL PETROLEUM CORP. Mobil Junior
Safety Economy Run for Elma High
School students. Hall's Mobil Station,
May 14, 1955.

PHOTO NO. 29315-R4-19

MOREHEAD MOTORS
STUDEBAKER-PACKARD
DEALER on Market Street near
Broadway in Aberdeen.
March 20, 1955.

MOREHEAD MOTORS maintenance shop for Studebaker and Packard automobiles in Aberdeen. March 20, 1955.

JOE RAMSEY MOTORS CHEVRON
STATION and Dodge-Plymouth
Dealership located at Simpson
Avenue and Oak Streets in
Aberdeen. August 7, 1959.

PHOTO NO. 14803

PHOTO NO. 3003

NEW ABERDEEN GARAGE MOBIL STATION and
Storage. Mobil gas pumps were wrecked when
driver lost control. October 8, 1955.

MOREHEAD MOTORS Edsel
Dealer located in the 100 block
of West Market Street.
August 24, 1957.

PHOTO NO. 32440

THE WASSON BUICK-CADILLAC agency service facilities in Aberdeen. September 20, 1957.

STAN HOOD CHEVRON SERVICE STATION in Aberdeen at Market and H Streets. Stan and wife Beverly receive United Air Line tickets for a Standard Oil Co. chartered Red Carpet flight to New York for about ten days training and entertainment seeing all the sights of the "Big Apple". Photograph taken September 4, 1956.

PHOTO NO. 32511

PHOTO NO. 31480

Hank Loman Signal Service Station at Simpson Avenue and 25th Street in Hoquiam, Washington on January 12, 1957. This place had a very large clientele for many years. It later became an Exxon Station. Poor health finally forced its closure.

Ralph Hovis' Chevron Station at Simpson Avenue and 28th Street in Hoquiam, August 28, 1957.

STANDARD OIL TANKER *W.H. Berg* maneuvering to the dock of the Standard Oil Co. tank farm at Aberdeen to unload a cargo of gasoline and fuel oil. When Super tankers replaced these smaller ships, the local supply had to then be transported by rail car or highway tank trucks. March 20, 1958.

WASSON BUICK-CADILLAC AGENCY in Aberdeen, September 20, 1957. Rumors had it that there were more Cadillacs per capita in Aberdeen than any other city in the United States. In the late 1920's there were about 23 large sawmills and all the families who were anybody drove Cadillacs.

RUDDACH MOTORS, Ford Agency in their new building on West Wishkah Street between Alder and Michigan Streets in Aberdeen in July of 1958.

ASSOCIATED TIDEWATER Flying "A" gas station owned by Paul Lisle located at Wishkah and K Streets in Aberdeen. Paul washes the windshield of a 1957 DeSota Fireflite. October 1, 1958.

UNION OIL COMPANY marine service dock, Ted Holand, Consignee, at the Port of Grays Harbor's Westport Marina. U. S. Coast Guard and Life Boat Station on the shore. Westport, Washington. November 21, 1959.

Union Oil Co. Tank Farm and Bulk Plant at Front and Dock Streets in Wesport, Washington. Ted Holand, consignee supplying Union Oil Co. Products to marine facilities Port of Grays Harbor Westhaven Marina. November 21, 1959.

Grand Opening of Union Oil '76 marine service for Westport, Washington Marina supplying Union Oil products for charter boats, commercial and pleasure craft as well as U. S. Coast Guard lifesaving facilities. Ted Holand, consignee. November 21, 1959.

Union '76 Station of Brumfield-Twidwell, Inc. Ford & Mercury dealership in Montesano, Washington at 301 Pioneer Avenue East, across the street from Larry's Mobil Station. August 1959.

STANDARD STATIONS, INC located at Wishkah and Broadway in Aberdeen, August 1, 1959. A new modern station was built around the old station so the operator wouldn't have to shut down service. Once the new station was built, the old metal and porcelain station was hauled to the scrap yard.

MOBIL FLYING RED HORSE SERVICE at the New Aberdeen Garage at Market and Broadway in Aberdeen. Ambulance and wrecker service along with auto storage facilities. July 25, 1959.

Lee's Texaco Station in Aberdeen located at Wishkah and G Street. Specializing in complete car care with Marfak Lubrication, Tires, Batteries and Washing along with two separate service areas. October 6, 1961.

Hank Loman's Signal Service Station at Simpson Avenue and 25th Street in Hoquiam, Washington. "John" displaying his trophy for winning the Soap Box Derby held in Aberdeen, July 19, 1961.

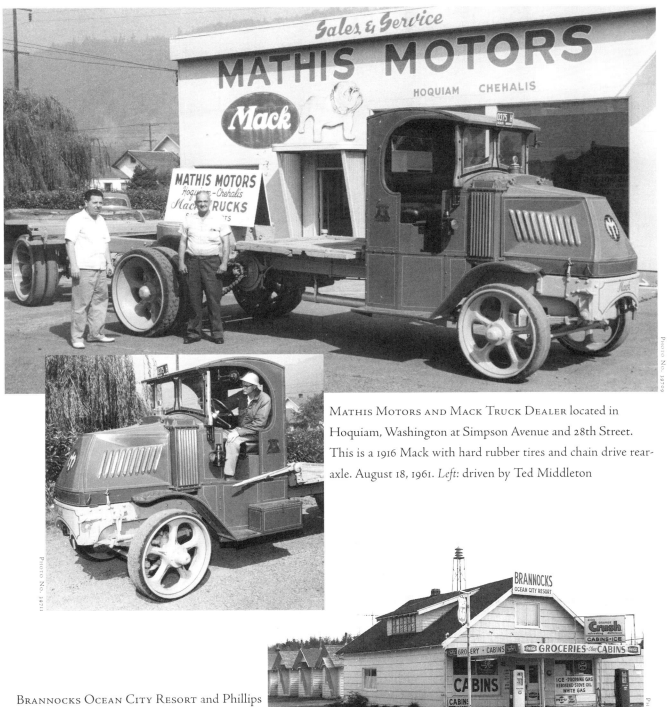

MATHIS MOTORS AND MACK TRUCK DEALER located in Hoquiam, Washington at Simpson Avenue and 28th Street. This is a 1916 Mack with hard rubber tires and chain drive rear-axle. August 18, 1961. *Left*: driven by Ted Middleton

BRANNOCKS OCEAN CITY RESORT and Phillips '66 gasoline pumps and cabin camp and grocery store at Ocean City, Washington. April 1968.

MOYER'S SHELL STATION at 201 West Curtis Street in Aberdeen, carrying gas and diesel and propane products. July 23, 1968.

PHOTO NO. 6147

PHOTO NO. 52359

PETROLANE BOTTLED GAS FIRE July 1, 1967. The plant was across the street from the Union '76 service station and the '76 ball melted from the intense heat of the raging fire. Several houses on the same side of the street as the service station were totally destroyed as well as the Petrolane Plant. The fire men had to keep pouring water on one tank that was about the size of a railroad tank car for fear it would explode and wipe out several blocks of structures.

ZIMMERMAN'S STANDARD OIL CHEVRON STATION in Aberdeen observing a student employee training program in operation by company managers and district supervisors. Station located at Broadway and Wishkah Street. October 1, 1962.

PHILLIPS '66 gas pumps at Dino's Central Park Grocery in Aberdeen, July 1, 1969.